Eros After Many Years

by

Paul J

Eros After Many Years

Poetry of the passion felt long ago and today. There is no greater love than that which I have for you.

Published by JM Publishing

For more information contact

Paul J
JM Publishing
36 Elm Street
Georgetown, MA 01833

ISBN 978-0-9907424-3-2

Love, After Many Years

Love still grows with each day
Even with each birthday.

You may call it comfortable, or
You may call it foolish

I will call it truth.

"I will love you until death parts us."

"Then there is an end?" she asked.

"Yes," I say
"To my life, there is an end.
My love is forever."

"You are right," she said.
"I will call it foolish …
And I will call it comfortable
Very comfortable
And sometimes I will call it an adventure, too."

Desire

Speak of her and speak of beauty
Look upon her and I know desire

Hair as black as raven's vestments
Falling across her snowy skin
So far beyond my reach she is
Her smile bids me enter in

I have no claim to her save love.
  Deserving of jewels,.of clothes, of wealth
   But I have none
  Charm and grace should greet her.
   But I have none.
My voice is lost
    Lost in her beauty.
  All that is good she deserves – All this and more.
   But I have none to offer

I have nothing to offer save my love

I have no claim, no claim to her

But she smiles again and says:
  "This is all the claim you need. All the claim you
will ever need."

Light

Light comes today
The sun behind clouds
Unseen except the light.

Is it necessary to be seen?
Is the light enough?
Is anything necessary at all?

She smiles at something foolish
She smiles at me
Light is not the same as the sun.

Paul J

Mary Enters

Soft light. Soft skin.
 Clothes lying upon it.
Limbs, body covered
 Enticing me the more to know.

My thought is beneath the cloth.

My thoughts explore, her skin, her flesh, my passion.
 Memory and future are one.
A different time. A different place.
 They are the same. The same now and to come.

She smiles; a smile like lightning
 Reaching toward me.
She knows my thought. She shares my thought.
 Thunder rumbles like passion caught in a moment.

The rumble of the thunder is like my love.
The thunder of love that follows the
lightning of lust.

The thunder rising within me
Deeper than cloth.
Deeper than skin.
Deeper than flesh.

With Mary the lightning and thunder come as one.
With her the lust and the love are one.
It should always be so.

The lust and the love.
The lightening and the thunder.
One and the same.
Complete.

The storm passes.
The love remains.

Paul J

Mary

There are men who are richer than me
But they do not have Mary

And there are many who are smarter than me
But they do not have Mary

Better athletes, more beautiful than me
But they do not have Mary

For all that they have, I hold no envy
For only I have Mary

Roses In April

Give me roses, though they will not last,
still give them to me.

Beauty never lasts. It fades as light fades and is buried

Faded and buried beneath;
beneath the fading memories of faded beauty.

Still give me roses while they last; while I last

While I am; I would have beauty for my companion.

Until the last, I would have beauty;
and mourn their pasting another day

Paul J

Saw Dust On the Wood

Wood cut -
    Saw drawn across it -
        To make, to change, to destroy.

This wood some god has made
    Ripped asunder by some other god
        To dust, to saw dust, by us.

All to make a thing that's new,
    Made from something that was newly made before
        Before the saw was made.
        Before we were made.
Cut wood to make these – the new, the old, the dust
    To make the saw dust on the wood.

The human hand changes and destroys
What was shaped, what was made
By the hand of another god.
.Cut to make new or just cut to prove
Who is the god? The maker of the wood
Or the maker of the dust?
The maker of saw dust?
Does God do this same thing?

Putting worlds beneath His saw.
Making new worlds of old worlds
Ripped apart to put together again
And we – We are the dust on the new world
Like the saw dust on the wood
Dust on His new world.

We are –
Saw dust on the wood.

Paul J

She Is

She moves beside me
      Soft and warm.
            Round and sensuous.
That shape that fills my dream complete,
Just as I have striven to fill her.

Her shape upon another's frame would be as sweet?
I think not, not ever, not in the least.

It is she alone that fills my dreams
      That fills my life
          That is my life.

She Walks With Me

We walk this earth with different strides.
I tread so slow when she would run.
And I hold straight when she strays far,
But still we end the walk as one.

The paths may twist and turn away
From where we once had set out sight.
New path would pull us both astray
To go on ways that are less right.

But I have learned to see in her,
And learn from her, and be in her.
For she is all the things I lack,
And what she needs, I have to share.

We are two, yet we are one.
We think as one. We move as one.
Though we are two, we are far more,
Then either one would be alone.

Paul J

Stay

Come lay with me
And breathe the breath I breathe
Dream the dream I dream
And share the thoughts I see

Share all that life will give
And share what life will take
Share all of this and stay
Stay until there is no more to share

Sweet Beneath

Sweet emptiness beneath the sheet
Where once did lie my love
Sweet breath she breathed, her scent so near
While she is far and gone

In thought we are together
Never parted long
Still the scent without the breath
Is only half a song

I will that she were with me
I will she'd never gone
But if she must, and truth that is
I will that she return

To lie beneath the sheet again
And warm me with her breath
And make her scent into the song
That we have sung so long.

Paul J

The Lightening and the Thunder

(revisited and revised)

She move as she always does, no difference
      The difference is in the seer, not the seen
The difference begins

She busies herself with tasks I do not notice
      Things of little consequence I would say if I did
notice
But I do not notice the things she does
      I notice her.

Our times passed. I remember them
      They are like this time, and when remembered
      Bring the burning to my thoughts
          Bring her past, our past into my thoughts.

Bring the flesh of a young body,
The fire of a young spirit
The needs of youth
These come back, but are put out of my mind
Put out by thoughts of the slow and smoldering
passion
Not the need of youth, but the desire of age.

She notices now. Notices my smile, my contemplation.

She knows she will have me.
No word is needed. She knew this when first she
moved

Soft swelling and sighs will follow the rhythm of flesh on
flesh.
Flesh warmed, satisfied, spent.
The need has passed, the desire answered.
That is how it will be -

But now it is the lust yet unanswered that comes
The lightening that comes,
Comes before the thunder

Paul J

Valentine's Day 2013

This one day is love?
One day each year?
For today we will speak
Of the love and the tear

Of love's passing
And of love's presence

Speak softly now, but stay
While all the others shout
Spend useless words today
But hold your passion out

Keep your passion
For all our days to come.

About the author

Paul J lives with his wife Mary, and writes poetry for her as he has done for forty two years. It is unlikely that he will stop now.

http://sobernowmusic.com/

http://pauljanson.com/

http://www.amazon.com/Paul-Janson/

www.ingramcontent.com/pod-product-compliance
Lightning Source LLC
Chambersburg PA
CBHW030013040426
42337CB00012BA/766